Flicker
Flash

10/00

DATE	ISSUED TO
SEP 26 2001	
NOV 19 2001	
FEB 27 2002	
MAY – 6 2002	
SEP 27 2002	
OCT 21 2002	
AUG 13 2003	

DEMCO 32-209

Flicker Flash

To Mom and Dad
Jim, Heather, and Aimee
family and friends
especially Shirley, Jane, Pat, and Mona—
thank you for lighting my way
—J. B. G.

To my parents
Thank you for encouraging me to follow my star.
—N. D.

Text copyright © 1999 by Joan Bransfield Graham
Illustrations copyright © 1999 by Nancy Davis

Library of Congress Cataloging-in-Publication Data

Graham, Joan Bransfield.
Flicker flash / Joan Bransfield Graham ; illustrated by Nancy Davis.
p. cm.
Summary: A collection of poems celebrating light in its various forms, from candles and lamps
to lightning and fireflies.
ISBN 0-395-90501-X
1. Light — Juvenile poetry. 2. Children's poetry, American. [1. Light — Poetry. 2. American
poetry.] I. Davis, Nancy, 1949–   ill. II. Title.
PS3557.R213F55   1999
811'.54 — dc21   98-12956 CIP AC

Manufactured in the United States of America
BVG 10 9 8 7 6 5 4 3

Flicker Flash

poems by **Joan Bransfield Graham**

illustrated by **Nancy Davis**

Light

Light,
light,
stretch
my sight,
bend back
c o r n e r s
of the night.
Flicker, flash,
near and far,
turn on lamps,
& sprinkle stars.
One small flame,
a tiny spark . . .
or wide as day,
you scatter dark.

Sun

"From 93,000,000 miles away I bring you this dynamite, ring-a-ding day. I'll shout in your window and bounce near your head to solar power you out of your bed!"

Candle

CANDLE

You
promise quick,
exotic light,
a dancing
vision of
the night,
you give
the room
a painted
face that
blinks and
winks and
helps erase
the feeling
of the empty
black that's
slyly creeping
up my back.

summer

earth
is spinning
toward the light,
first it's day,
and then it's
night

around the sun

all winter spring
in one big swing

Firefly

Firefly,
flit
high
THEN
do you
know
LOW
what
makes
you
GLOW?

Crescent Moon

new   grin

moon   night

sliver   the

thin   see

nice to

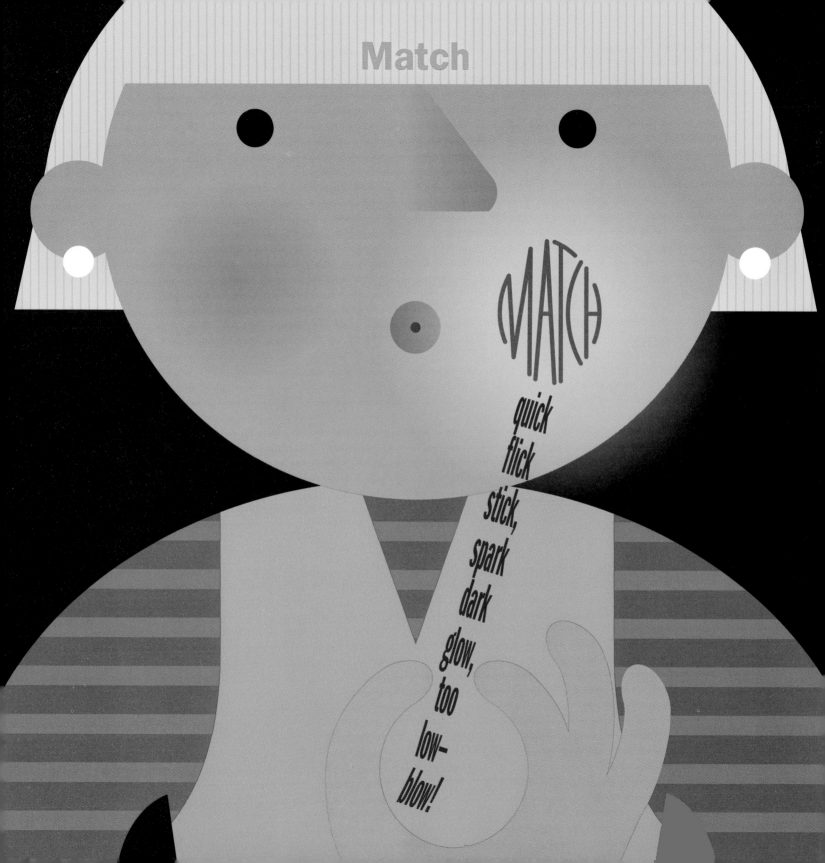

MATCH
quick
flick
stick,
spark
dark
glow,
too
low—
blow!

Birthday Candles

Happy Day Happy Year

Like shooting stars that blaze the dark, you flame — then disappear. But when I look, I see your light in faces, circled near.

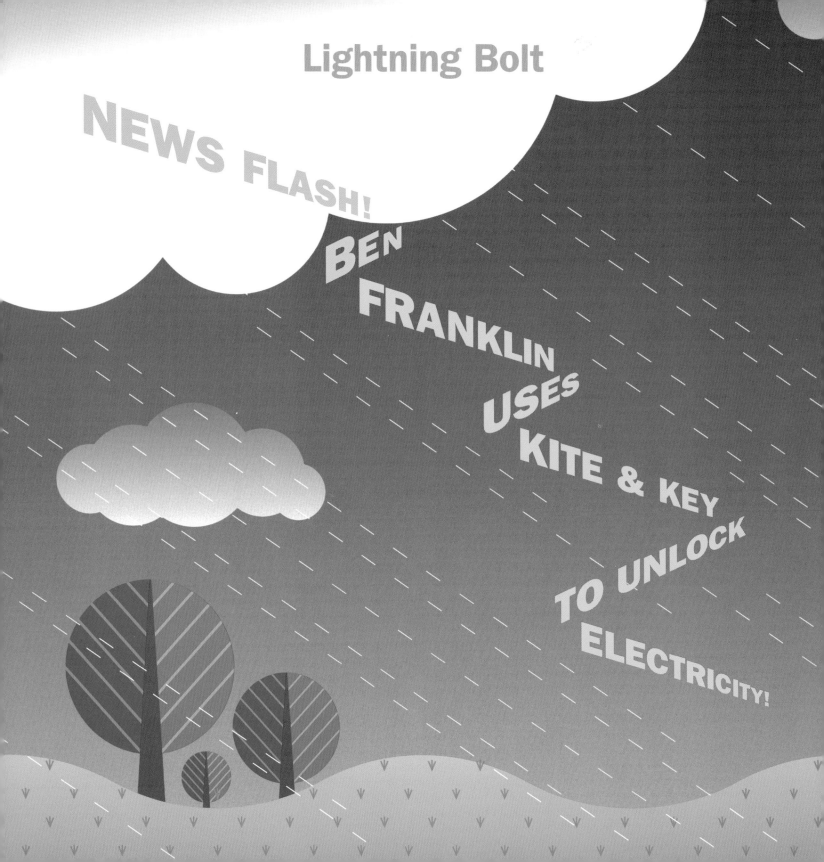

Light Bulb

Thomas
Edison didn't
hesitate to let
ideas incubate, and
try again, if they
weren't right. One
day to his intense
delight, he squeezed
his thoughts
into a bulb
and then
turned
on the
light
light
light
!!!

Porch Light

I spread a welcome mat of light across the doorstep of the night.

WELCOME   WELCOME
WE MEET AGAIN
WELCOME   WELCOME
PLEASE COME IN

Stars

in
space

star
mail

can
seem

quite
slow

this card
was sent

Full Moon

like
a *MIRROR*,
far away, moon
REFLECTS the
flames of day, in
a *SILVER* kind
of way

ago

light
years

Television

a luminous square box brings light through wires and air, shows superheroes save the world while I'm just s i t t i n g there

Refrigerator Light

Open the door.

By
the
light
in the
refrigerator,
I can plainly see
that the Brussels
sprouts are meant
for Y O U . . . the
chocolate cake's
for ME.

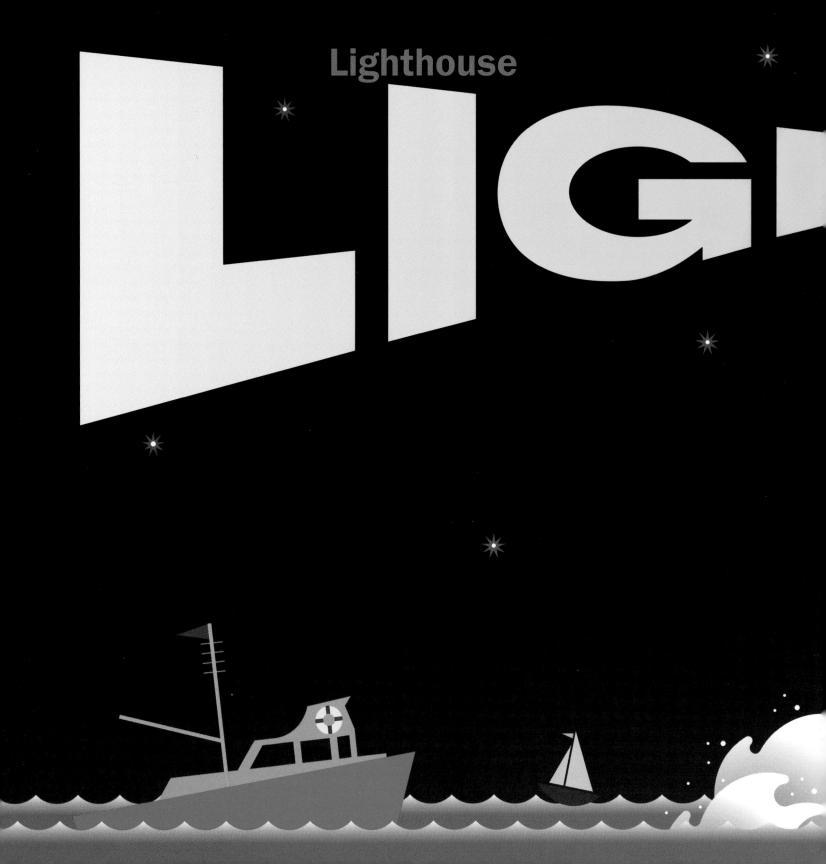

Lighthouse

LIGH

Oh,
Captain
of the
midnight
sky, you
stretch
your arms
and flash
your eye
across the
waves and
churning
foam to
steer me,
guide me,
safely
HOME.

LIGHT
HOUSE

**Warm
as a hen,
this toasty
trick will turn
an egg into
a chick!**

PEEP
PEEP

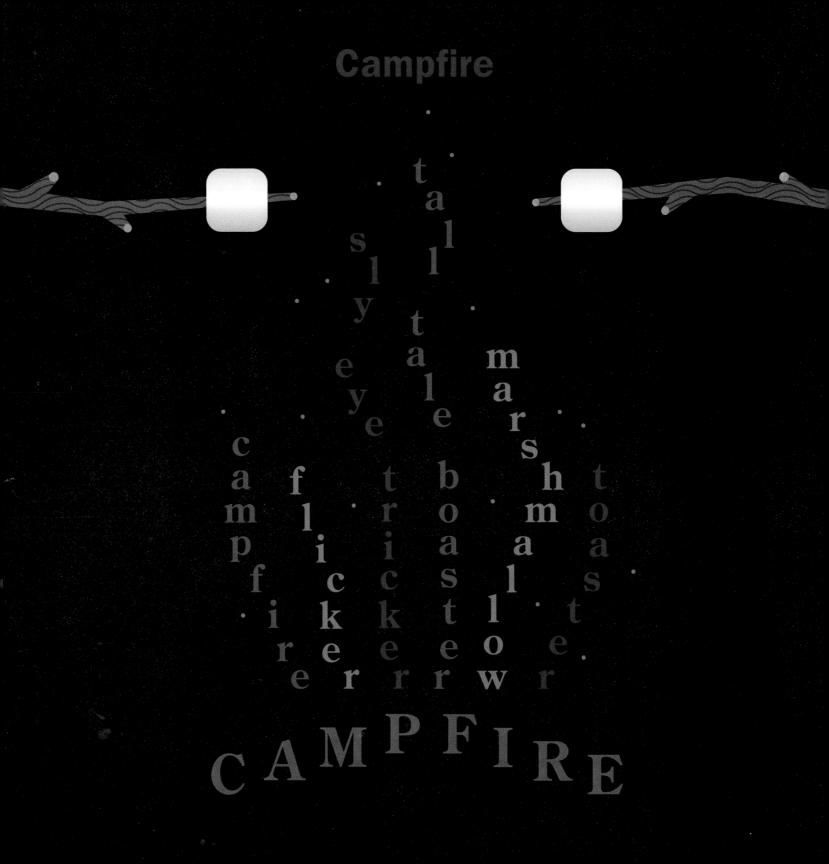

Flashlight

click
one flick
I am the SUN,
I chase the shadows
one by one, growing scary,
jagged, tall – with brilliant beams
I'll MELT them ALL!

shooting up high, scattering petals across the sky?

Lamp

soft gold
lamp-shine makes
this book *all mine*, in
this welcome curve of light,
nestled in the lap of night

L
A
M
P
L A M P